*For Adults*

# — introduction —

I n this book of seven classic children's stories, I have taken some of the original stories and placed them in the time of my childhood. I have made the stories modern, funny, and about the arts. I found the French word *Fabliaux* in the dictionary and thought it fit. *Fabliaux* is defined as short, usually comic, coarse, and cynical tales in verse popular in the 12th and 13th centuries. After I wrote the stories, I had the idea to use my prints from Crown Point Press as illustrations. I changed my writing slightly to accommodate the prints and turn the book into a vehicle for giving the prints a new life by incorporating them into the stories.

I would like to thank Kathan Brown for advice and editing, Sasha Baguskas for preparing the images, Brent Jones for his book design, and all the people who buy this book and the prints that are illustrated.

—Tom Marioni

SHORT, COMIC, COARSE, CYNICAL TALES IN VERSE

# FABLiAUX

## —Tom Marioni Fairy Tales—

ISBN 978-1-891300-22-6
Published by Crown Point Press
Printed in China through Colorcraft Ltd., Hong Kong
Book design by Brent A. Jones

Cover image: *American Eagle*, 1994

# TABLE OF CONTENTS

# RIP VAN WINKLE
## — ART HISTORY —

In the year of our Lord nineteen hundred and forty seven,
One year before the television revolution of Uncle Milty,
One year before George Orwell wrote *1984* and one year before Cadillacs had fins,
There was a radio program called Rip Predicts.
The star of the show had been asleep for twenty years.
According to his wife, he had been a good-for-nothing lazy dreamer.
He would sit under his favorite tree every morning and make sketches of fantasy machines
  and dream of flying in space with all his no-account friends.

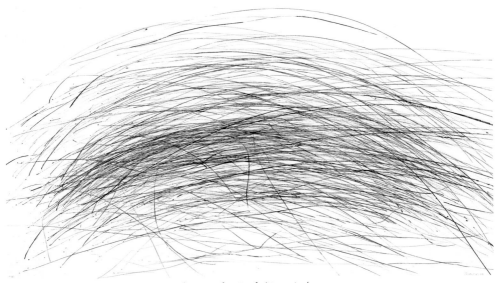

*Flying with Friends (Drypoint)*, 2000

Rip Van Winkle had fallen asleep under a tree in 1927 in the middle of the flapper era
Just two years before the big crash of 1929.
He had slept all through the Depression, and the Second World War.
When he awoke in a new world in 1947 he saw so many advances in technology:
Radar, jet planes, the atomic bomb, ballpoint pens,
Vitamin pills, electric stoves, dishwashers, and pegged pants.
Based on knowledge of his time, fresh in his mind, he could see patterns in history.
This gave him the ability to predict the future.

Tastes and styles went in and out of favor every other decade.

The art style of the '40s was realistic, the '50s abstract, the '60s realistic, the '70s abstract, the '80s realistic, and on and on every other decade.

Rip could see that events in the world went in cycles.

*Feather Circle,* 1986

The oppressed became the oppressors, our enemies became our friends.

Neighborhoods that were poor became rich and vice versa.

On the first broadcast of the radio show, Rip predicted a Catholic president in 13 years, and that a hillbilly would invent a style of music stolen from negro blues music.

These predictions were considered ridiculous but the show got high ratings.

It became a popular comedy show. Every new prediction brought on new controversies, along with an ever increasing audience coast to coast.

Each week Rip would go into a trance by drumming on the table that held the microphone and come up with the next prediction on the spot.

*Drumming,* 2002

The home audience would become hypnotized by the trance drumming
and hang on his every word.

The predictions were coming faster each week.

The German mark and the Japanese yen would be flying high by the 1980s,
and later collapse. In another two decades the dollar would collapse.

*Flying Yen,* 1990

When Rip Van Winkle predicted social unrest and a drug culture in the 1960s,
   death threats were sent to the station.
He predicted that science would prove the Bible wrong and there would be a religious
   backlash in the entire world, with religious wars fought over whether
   my god could beat up your god.

*Cross*, 1982

By the end of 1947, the public could not take it any more, and the show was no longer funny.
It was canceled and Rip went into seclusion at the corner tavern.

THE END

I n the 1950s, there was a girl with blonde hair who wore horn-rimmed glasses.
She was tall, had a great body, was up-town smart and creative.
She went to art school and studied design and drawing.
One day she was riding her bicycle in the country on a dirt road in the hills of Marin County.
On a hill overlooking the ocean she spotted a modern house.
The house had a long patio with a yellow awning over it.

*Golden Rectangle,* 2003